CHARLIE BROWN'S CYCLOPEDIA

OUR INCREDIBLE UNIVERSE
From Stars to Black Holes

VOLUME · 9 ·

Based on the Charles M. Schulz Characters
Funk & Wagnalls

Charlie Brown's 'Cyclopedia
has been produced
by Mega-Books of New York,
Inc. in conjunction
with the editorial, design,
and marketing staff of
Field Publications.

STAFF FOR MEGA-BOOKS

Pat Fortunato
Editorial Director

Diana Papasergiou
Production Director

Susan Lurie
Executive Editor

Rosalind Noonan
Senior Editor

Adam Schmetterer
Research Director

**Michaelis/Carpelis
Design Assoc., Inc.**
Art Direction and Design

STAFF FOR FIELD PUBLICATIONS

Cathryn Clark Girard
Assistant Vice President,
Juvenile Publishing

Elizabeth Isele
Executive Editor

Kristina Jones
Executive Art Director

Leslie Erskine
Marketing Manager

Elizabeth Zuraw
Senior Editor

Michele Italiano-Perla
Group Art Director

Kathleen Hughes
Senior Art Director

Photo and Illustration Credits:
Jet Propulsion Laboratory, 39, 42, 44, 45, 46; Bryce Lee, 14, 16, 20, 21, 29, 40, 51; John Lemker/Earth Scenes, 26, 37; C.C. Lockwood/Earth Scenes, 17; NASA, 24, 40, 42, 43; National Optical Astronomy Observatories, 34, 49; Mary Ellen Senor, 18, 21, 24, 28, 33, 36, 52, 54.

Copyright © 1990, 1980 United Features Syndicate, Inc. Produced in association with Charles M. Schulz Creative Associates. All rights reserved under Universal and Pan-American copyright conventions. Published in the United States by Funk & Wagnalls L. P., Ramsey, New Jersey. Distributed by Funk & Wagnalls L. P., Ramsey, New Jersey and Field Publications Limited Partnership, Middletown, Connecticut. Manufactured in the United States of America.

ISBN: 0-8374-0054-6

Part of the material in this volume was previously published in *Charlie Brown's Second Super Book of Questions and Answers*.

Funk & Wagnalls, founded in 1876, is the publisher of *Funk & Wagnalls New Encyclopedia*, one of the most widely owned home and school reference sets, and many other adult and juvenile educational publications.

INTRODUCTION

Welcome to volume 9 of *Charlie Brown's 'Cyclopedia!* Have you ever wondered how a star is born, or what the weather is like on Neptune, or where a black hole is found? Charlie Brown and the rest of the *Peanuts* gang are here to help you find the answers to these questions and many more about your universe. Have fun!

CONTENTS

Look up into the night sky. The Moon glows brightly, and, as far as your eyes can see, the stars sparkle like tiny diamonds. What lies beyond the Earth, the Moon, and the stars, which seem to go on forever? Let's take a trip through our incredible universe and find out!

YOUR AMAZING UNIVERSE

LET'S MEET THE UNIVERSE—GALAXIES AND OUR SOLAR SYSTEM

What is the universe?

The word *universe* means everything there is—the Moon, the Sun, the Earth, the other planets, the stars, and anything else you can think of. All of space and everything in space is part of the universe. It extends much, much farther than you could see with the most powerful of all telescopes. Most scientists believe that there is an end to the universe, but no one knows where the end is.

How did the universe form?

Most scientists believe the universe began with a giant explosion—a big bang. This probably happened between 10 and 20 billion years ago. Before the explosion, all the material or "matter" in the universe was packed together tightly. The explosion blew it apart, sending hot gases and matter flying in every direction! After hundreds of millions of years, galaxies were formed from the swirling gases of the explosion. Later, stars and planets formed from the gases remaining in each galaxy.

THERE ARE SO MANY STARS AND PLANETS...IT'S HARD TO KEEP TRACK OF THEM!

Outer space is filled with faint radio waves. Some scientists believe these are the dying radio echoes of the Big Bang!

What is a star made of?

When you look up at the sky on a clear night, you see many, many twinkling stars. These points of light are really huge balls of bright, hot, glowing gases. They pour out light, just the way the Sun does. In fact, the Sun *is* a star. The other stars look much smaller than the Sun because they are much farther away from the Earth.

What is a galaxy?

A galaxy is a huge cluster of stars held close together by gravity. "Close together" for stars means they're actually billions of miles apart! Through a telescope, galaxies look like islands. Each one contains billions of stars. Scientists don't know how many galaxies there are in the universe, but they believe there may be 100 billion!

If you counted one star per second, it would take you more than 12,000 years to count the 400 billion stars in a normal galaxy!

What galaxy is Earth in?

Our own star—the Sun—and the Earth and other planets are all part of the Milky Way galaxy. From one part of space, far beyond our galaxy, the whole galaxy would appear as one big band of light with a bulge in the middle. From another part of space beyond our galaxy, the Milky Way would appear as a glowing spiral-shaped island. Our own Sun would appear as a medium-sized star on one of the spiral's starry arms.

If you looked at the night sky from a place far from city lights, you might see the Milky Way as a glowing band of light stretching across the sky. This band is made up of billions of stars. You cannot see the separate stars in the band without using a telescope because the stars are so far away from us.

The glowing band is actually only part of the galaxy that we call the Milky Way. This galaxy includes all the separate stars we see in the night sky. These stars are closer to the Earth than the band is, so we don't see them all blurred together.

THE MILKY WAY

What is a solar system?

A solar system is a family of planets and other objects that orbit, or travel around, a star. That star is a Sun. The Sun's family consists of planets, asteroids, comets, and meteors. Many scientists think that there could be planets orbiting many stars. This would mean that there are many solar systems!

What is our solar system?

The Sun and all the objects that orbit it—including the Earth—form our solar system. The Sun is at the center of our solar system. The Sun's gravity is a pulling force much stronger than the gravity of Earth. The Sun's gravity, along with the movement of each planet, keeps the planets in their paths around the Sun. Without the Sun's gravity, each planet would fly off into space. Without its own path, each planet would fall into the Sun!

CHAPTER 2

From space it looks like a big blue marble. Scientists think it's the only planet in the solar system that has living beings. It's also the only planet with flowing water on its surface. Have you guessed which planet we're talking about? It's your very own home—Earth!

NO PLACE LIKE HOME

HOME SWEET HOME

EARTH FACTS

When was the Earth formed?

Many scientists believe that the Earth was probably formed about five billion years ago. At first the Earth's air was poisonous, and there was no life. Over billions of years, the Earth changed. Now the Earth provides the energy, warmth, water, and air we need to keep us alive.

How big is the Earth?

If you could dig a tunnel through the center of the Earth from one side to the other, your tunnel would be almost 8,000 miles long. That distance is greater than 140,000 football fields placed end to end. If you walked around the Earth, you'd have to walk almost 25,000 miles—some 440,000 football fields!

Even though the Earth seems like a very big place, the Sun is much bigger. The Sun is 108 times wider than the Earth. It's so much bigger than the Earth that you could fit more than one million planets the size of the Earth inside the Sun!

In the sixth century B.C., a man named Pythagoras (pi-THAG-or-us) claimed that the Earth was shaped like a ball. Most people didn't believe him. They thought the Earth was flat!

How much does Earth weigh?

Our planet weighs about 6,600 million trillion tons.

What star is closest to Earth?

The Sun is our closest star. Other stars look much smaller than the Sun because they are much farther away from the Earth. Actually, many other stars in our universe are bigger than the Sun.

The Sun is actually a star.

How far is the Earth from the Sun?

The Sun is 93 million miles away from us. That may sound very far away, but it takes only eight minutes for the Sun's light to reach us. The Sun is close enough to give the Earth light and heat.

If the Sun were the size of a large orange, the Earth would be the size of a tiny seed about 33 feet away!

WHEN WILL HE REALIZE HE'LL NEVER KICK THAT BALL OFF THE EARTH!

boot! boot! boot! boot! boot! boot!

Why can't a football fall off the Earth?

A football, or any other object, cannot fall off the Earth because it is always pulled toward the Earth by gravity. This invisible force draws all things on the Earth toward its center.

THE EARTH RACING THROUGH SPACE

How long does it take the Earth to orbit the Sun?

The Earth takes a little more than 365 days to orbit the Sun. That's how long one year lasts on the Earth.

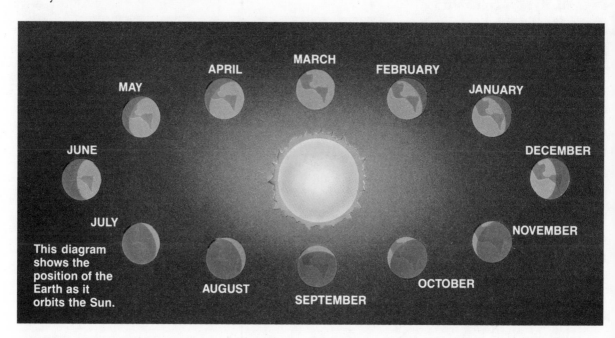

MARCH · APRIL · MAY · JUNE · JULY · FEBRUARY · JANUARY · DECEMBER · NOVEMBER · OCTOBER · SEPTEMBER · AUGUST

This diagram shows the position of the Earth as it orbits the Sun.

How fast does the Earth travel around the Sun?

Scientists have figured out that the Earth is racing through space at about 67,000 miles an hour—thousands of times faster than the fastest racing car. During the time it took you to read this answer, the Earth probably moved through space more than 300 miles!

IT SAYS HERE THAT THE WORLD REVOLVES AROUND THE SUN ONCE A YEAR..

THE WORLD REVOLVES AROUND THE SUN?

ARE YOU SURE?

I THOUGHT IT REVOLVED AROUND ME!

Why don't you feel the Earth moving?

You can't feel the Earth moving through space because it moves so smoothly. When you ride in a car, you know you're moving, even if you close your eyes. That's because the ride is bumpy. When you are on a jet plane and you close your eyes, most of the time you cannot tell the plane is moving. That's because the ride is smooth. The movement of the Earth through space is even smoother, so you cannot feel it at all.

The Earth is moving with the Sun and the rest of the solar system through space. Because of this motion, even though we are carried around the Sun year after year, the Earth never returns to the same place in space twice!

AXIS

What makes the Sun rise?

The Sun doesn't rise; the Earth turns. The Earth is always turning on its axis, an imaginary line that goes through the North and South poles. This motion of the Earth on its axis is called rotation (row-TAY-shun).

What happens when the Earth rotates?

If you have a globe and a flashlight, you can do an experiment to see why the Sun seems to rise. Place a lamp or flashlight so that it shines on the globe. Pretend that the light is sunlight. You can see that the light is hitting only one part of the globe. Now turn the globe slowly. As the globe turns, a different part of the globe is lighted. In the same way, as the Earth turns, a different part of the Earth gets sunlight. When the side of the Earth you live on isn't facing the Sun, you have night. When the Earth turns farther around, the part you live on comes into the sunlight. Then the Sun seems to rise in the sky, and you have daylight. Because the Earth rotates, the stars also seem to rise and set like the Sun. For the same reason, you also see the Moon rise and set.

If the Earth didn't move, half of the world would always be in sunlight, and the other half would always be dark. Aren't you glad that the Earth rotates?

NOT SO FAST, SNOOPY!

The ancient Egyptians believed that the Sun hatched each day from the egg of a heavenly goose!

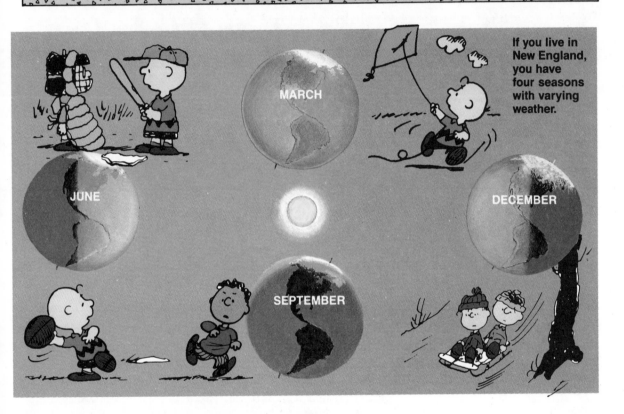

If you live in New England, you have four seasons with varying weather.

MARCH

JUNE

DECEMBER

SEPTEMBER

Why do we have seasons?

As you've learned, it takes a year for the Earth to make one trip around the Sun. The Earth's axis doesn't point straight up and down, so the Earth tilts to one side as it travels around the Sun. This tilt gives us our four seasons.

In summer, when the part of the Earth you live on tilts toward the Sun, you get the most hours of sunlight and heat. In the fall, your part of the Earth begins to tilt away from the Sun, and you get less sunlight and heat. In winter, when your part of the Earth tilts still farther away from the Sun, you get even less sunlight and heat. In the spring, your part of the Earth tilts closer to the Sun again, and you get more hours of sunlight and heat.

CHAPTER 3

THE MOON UP CLOSE

Ready to go next door for a visit? Next door in space, that is! The Moon is Earth's closest neighbor. You can see it glowing in the sky most nights, and some Earthlings have even traveled there already. Would you like to take a journey to the Moon? Well, come along!

MOON FACTS

Where did the Moon come from?

According to many scientists, the Moon could have been formed in several ways. One possibility is that both the Earth and Moon may have formed about five billion years ago, with the larger Earth "capturing" the smaller Moon in its gravity. Another possibility is that the Moon formed from some kind of collision of two larger planets when the solar system first began five billion years ago. Scientists don't know which idea is right, but many believe that the age of the Earth and Moon are the same—about five billion years.

How big is the Moon?

The Moon might look large when it's full, but the Earth is almost four times larger. Even so, the Moon is almost as wide as the United States. A tunnel through the Moon would be 2,160 miles long!

I GUESS IT'S A LITTLE TOO FAR TO WALK THERE.

How far from the Earth is the Moon?

The Moon is about 239,000 miles away from the Earth. That's almost 80 times the distance between New York and California!

Why does the Moon shine?

The Moon does not shine with its own light. It has no light to give out. The Moon reflects, or sends back, light rays that come to it from the Sun. Those light rays reach the Earth—and your eyes.

Just as the Sun shines on part of the Earth at all times, the Sun shines on part of the Moon at all times. The Moon is always reflecting some sunlight, but you cannot always see it. During the day, the Sun shines on the part of the Earth where you live. The Sun's light is brighter than the Moon's light, so the sunlight usually hides the Moon from your sight. At night, no sunlight hides the Moon, so you can see it "shining" unless it's hidden by clouds.

The Sun's rays bounce off not only the Moon, but also the Earth. If you were out in space, you would see the Earth shining more brightly than the Moon!

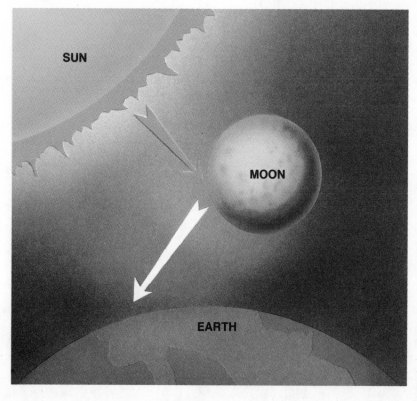

Light rays from the Sun bounce off the Moon, which enables us to see the Moon from Earth.

SUN

MOON

EARTH

What does the Moon look like close up?

The Moon is very rough and rocky. It has tall mountains, deep cracks, and steep cliffs. All over the Moon are thousands of deep holes shaped like saucers. These holes are called craters. Many of them were formed when rocks flying through space crashed into the Moon. Most of these flying rocks were moving so fast that they shattered when they hit the Moon. Bits of them were scattered all over, so you cannot find the rocks, but you can see the holes they made. Some craters are less than a foot wide. Others are nearly 150 miles wide.

I THINK YOU STEPPED IN A CRATER, SIR.

The crater Copernicus is one of the easiest craters on the Moon for us to see. The bottom of the crater is nearly 50 miles across. The mountains at the rim of the crater are nearly 12,000 feet high, a climb of more than 2 miles for a future astronaut!

What are the dark areas on the Moon's surface?

The dark areas we have discovered on the surface of the Moon are called *maria*, which means seas. But these seas aren't like the seas on Earth. Billions of years ago, large asteroids hit the surface of the Moon. This created huge basins or holes. Many years later, these basins were filled with melted rock. When this rock cooled on the Moon's surface, it formed these dark spots. Some spots are very big. The largest is about 700 miles across.

A closeup view of the Moon.

Small moonquakes rock the Moon about 3,000 times every year!

THERE IT GOES AGAIN!

Can anything live on the Moon?

Because the Moon has no air or water, people, plants, and animals cannot live there. American astronauts have visited the Moon by bringing supplies with them. However, scientists have found that, with air and water, plants can grow in Moon soil that the astronauts brought back to Earth.

THE MOON IN MOTION

Why do we see only one side of the Moon?

Just as the Earth moves in two different ways, the Moon also moves in two different ways. It turns on its axis, and it travels in its orbit around the Earth. The Moon takes 27 days, 7 hours, and 43 minutes to turn around once on its axis—about the same amount of time it takes the Moon to travel once around the Earth. This means that the Moon always keeps the same side facing the Earth. From the Earth you never see the other side of the Moon.

Does the Moon really control the ocean's tides?

Yes, it does. The Moon has its own gravity, just as the Earth and all other planets do. The Moon's pull on the Earth isn't strong enough for us to notice on land, although there are instruments that can measure it. We do see its effect on the seas, however. As the Moon travels around the Earth, its gravity pulls up the seas. When that happens, we say it is high tide. As the Moon passes away, the seas flow back to low tide.

YOU JUST CAN'T TAKE YOUR EYES OFF OF ME, CAN YOU SCHROEDER?

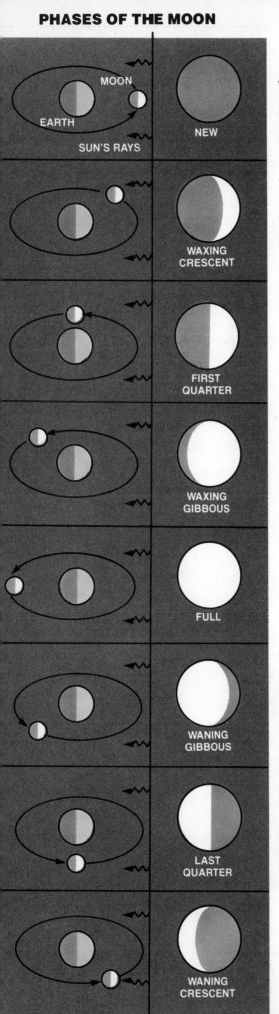

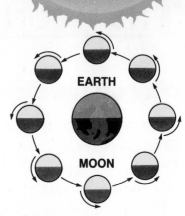

SUN

Why doesn't the Moon always look round?

As we've learned, the Moon has no light of its own. Light comes to it from the Sun, just as light comes to the Earth from the Sun. A part of the Moon is always turned toward the Sun, and a part of it is always turned away from the Sun. One part is as dark as night. The other part is as bright as day. We see the Moon only when some of the lighted part is turned toward the Earth.

As the Moon travels around the Earth, it always keeps the same side facing the Earth. We can't always see all of that side, however, because different amounts of it are lighted by the Sun during different days of the month. Sometimes, then, we see just a sliver. Sometimes we see a half Moon, and sometimes we see a full Moon.

The different shapes of the Moon are called phases. The Moon goes through all its phases every 29 to 30 days.

No one had seen the far side of the Moon until 1959, when a Soviet spacecraft took the first photos of it!

AN ECLIPSE OF THE MOON

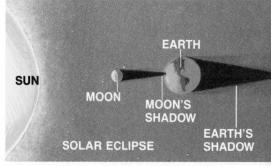

What causes an eclipse of the Moon?

When the Sun shines on them, the Earth and Moon cast shadows into space. An eclipse of the Moon happens when the Moon moves behind the Earth and into the Earth's shadow. Because the Moon is in this shadow, most of the Sun's light cannot hit the Moon, and you can barely see it. What you do see of the Moon looks reddish. When the Moon comes out from the Earth's shadow, it shines again with full light from the Sun. The eclipse is over.

Can the Moon's shadow cause an eclipse of the Sun?

Yes, it can. Even though the Moon is much smaller than the Sun, it is so close to us that when the Moon moves directly in front of the Sun, it blocks the Sun's light, and casts a shadow on part of the Earth. If you are in one of those shadowy places, you see an eclipse—the round disk of the Moon passing across the face of the Sun.

Because looking straight at the Sun can harm your eyes, you should never do it—even during an eclipse. Scientists who study eclipses have special equipment which allows them to view an eclipse of the Sun safely. Eclipses of the Moon are not dangerous to look at.

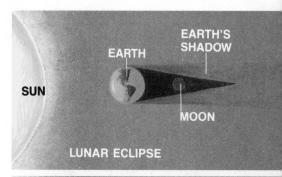

What's the difference between a total eclipse and a partial eclipse?

Total eclipse means that the whole Sun or the whole Moon is blocked from view. Partial eclipse means that only a part of the Moon or the Sun is blocked out. Partial eclipses happen when the Earth, Moon, and Sun do not line up exactly.

29

CHAPTER · 4

Our Sun is only one of billions of stars in our galaxy, but it's very important to us. After all, without the Sun's rays, we wouldn't have any light or heat! What would you see if you could travel close to the Sun? Let's discover the Sun's secrets.

OUR MIGHTY SUN

SUN FACTS

What is the Sun made of?

Hydrogen and helium are the two main gases that make up the Sun. Hydrogen is the Sun's fuel. Every second, millions of tons of hydrogen in the Sun's center, or core, change into helium. This change, called nuclear fusion, releases lots of energy.

How hot is the Sun?

The temperature of the outer part of the Sun is about 10,000 degrees Fahrenheit. Any metal known on Earth would melt at such a high temperature. Most other things on Earth would burn up. The inside of the Sun is even hotter than the outside. Scientists think that the temperature at the Sun's center is about 27 million degrees Fahrenheit.

Where does the Sun's energy go?

After many years, energy released in the Sun's core rises to its surface and travels into space. Part of this energy becomes our sunshine, which takes a little more than eight minutes to reach the Earth!

Never look directly at the Sun. The strong light can easily blind you!

LOOK, CHUCK, IT'S AURORA BOREALIS, NATURE'S GREAT LIGHT SHOW!

What is solar wind?

The Sun gives off a stream of gases flowing out in all directions. This is called solar wind. This wind travels all the way through our solar system. It even blows beyond Pluto, the planet that is farthest from the Sun.

The Earth is usually protected from solar wind by two magnetic belts. When there's lots of activity on the Sun's surface, however, some particles do get through to reach the Earth. When these particles collide with particles in the atmosphere near the North and South poles of the Earth, a glowing effect called an aurora (ah-ROAR-ah) occurs. Auroras create a beautiful colored light show in the Earth's sky. In the Northern Hemisphere, this show of lights is called the aurora borealis (ah-ROAR-ah bore-ee-AL-is).

Does the Sun rotate in space?

The Sun rotates on its own axis, but it doesn't do so in the same way that our Earth does. Gases in the middle of the Sun rotate faster than those at the top and bottom do.

The Sun takes more than 25 days to rotate once at its middle, while gases at the top and bottom rotate once in nearly 29 days! Our Earth is solid, so all of it rotates every 24 hours.

ON THE SURFACE OF THE SUN

What is the surface of the Sun like?

The Sun's surface swirls with hot gases. Sometimes, long streams of gas shoot out, then loop back to the Sun's surface. These arch-shaped fountains of burning gas are called prominences (PROM-ih-nen-sez).

The greatest prominence ever recorded shot 250,000 miles from the surface of the Sun! That's more than the distance between the Moon and the Earth!

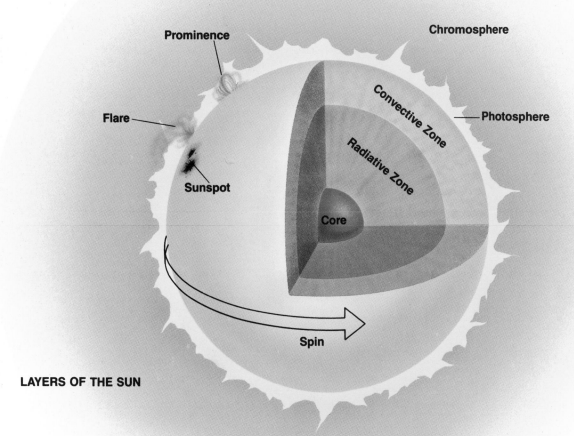

Prominence

Chromosphere

Flare

Convective Zone

Radiative Zone

Photosphere

Sunspot

Core

Spin

LAYERS OF THE SUN

What are sunspots?

Sunspots are dark patches on the surface of the Sun. These spots are cooler than the rest of the Sun's surface, so they shine less brightly. They may last only a few hours or as long as a few weeks.

Eight Earths can fit into the area of one of the larger sunspots!

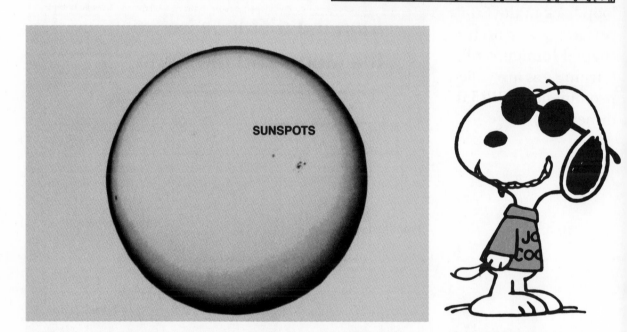

SUNSPOTS

How do scientists study the Sun's surface?

Since looking directly at the Sun can damage your eyes, scientists study the Sun by using special instruments that reflect its light. The McMath Telescope in Arizona is one of these instruments. It is the world's largest solar telescope.

Each day, a large mirror at the top of a tower reflects sunlight down a long tunnel to an underground room. There, another mirror reflects the Sun's image to a special observing room. In this room, scientific instruments are kept at a cool, constant temperature because the intense heat of the Sun's rays could damage them. Even small changes in temperature would upset the instruments used to study the Sun.

By studying the Sun, scientists hope to find out what makes its energy change from day to day, and how the Sun's energy affects life on Earth.

CHAPTER 5

Ready to explore? The planets in space have so many secrets to reveal. So zip up your space suit and follow the *Peanuts* gang on an exciting voyage through our solar system. We'll start at the planet closest to the Sun. First stop: Mercury!

THE FAMILY OF THE SUN

SPACE TRAVEL AGENCY

THE AGENT IS IN

SOLAR SYSTEM FACTS

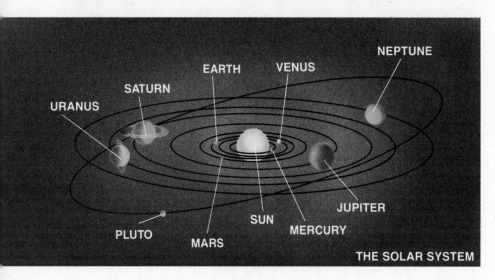

THE SOLAR SYSTEM

NEPTUNE
EARTH VENUS
SATURN
URANUS
PLUTO
MARS
SUN
MERCURY
JUPITER

What are the names of the planets in the solar system?

The planet closest to the Sun is called Mercury. Then come Venus, Earth, Mars, Jupiter, Saturn, Uranus, Neptune and Pluto.

Does the solar system move?

Yes. The Sun and all its planets are traveling around the center of our galaxy. The whole solar system is moving at the speed of 175 miles a second around the center of the Milky Way galaxy!

THAT'S GRAVITY FOR YOU!

Is the Earth the only planet with gravity?

No. Each planet has gravity. That means that Mars pulls things toward its center. Pluto pulls things toward its center. So do Saturn, Jupiter, and all the others. In fact, everything in the universe has gravity—even a pencil and a grain of sand. Of course, the bigger the object is, the stronger its pull. A tiny satellite doesn't have much gravity, so a spaceship at equal distance between a planet and a satellite would be pulled toward the planet. Stars have the greatest gravity because they are bigger than any other objects in the universe. The Sun's strong pull keeps the planets in orbit around it.

Can we see any of the nine planets without a telescope?

THE MOON

VENUS

Yes, we can see Saturn, Mercury, Venus, Mars, and Jupiter. Mercury is hard to see because it is often close to the Sun and hidden by its glare. You can usually tell when you're looking at a planet in the night sky because it shines with a bright, steady light. The planets, except for Mercury, don't twinkle the way stars do.

Sometimes planets such as Venus appear as stars in the night sky.

Some scientists have been able to see Uranus without a telescope because they know exactly where to look in the sky. They also make their observations far from city lights, where the sky is clear and dark!

The first star you see in the night sky may not be a star at all. It could be a planet—either Mercury, Venus, Mars, Jupiter, or Saturn!

Which of the planets, besides Earth, have moons?

Mars has 2 moons called Phobos and Deimos. Jupiter has 16 moons. Scientists have seen 17 moons around Saturn, 15 around Uranus, and 8 around Neptune. The farthest planet, Pluto, has 1 moon. Each moon travels in an orbit around its planet.

STARLIGHT, STAR BRIGHT, FIRST STAR I SEE TONIGHT. WISH I MAY. WISH I MIGHT. HAVE THE WISH I WISH TONIGHT.

DON'T TELL HIM IT'S A PLANET!

Mercury, Venus, and Mars

What are the inner planets?

Mercury, Venus, and Mars, along with the Earth, are sometimes called the inner planets because they are the nearest to the Sun. These four planets also have something else in common. All are solid, with rocky surfaces.

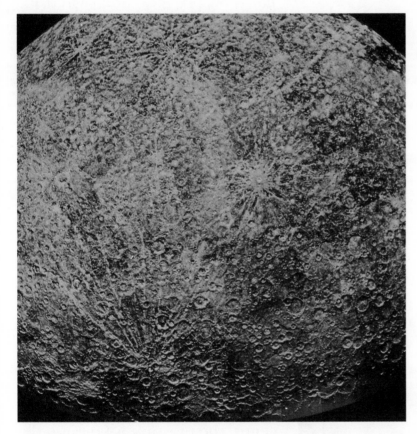

Which planet orbits the Sun the fastest?

Mercury. It travels at about 108,000 miles an hour, and makes one complete orbit of the Sun every three months.

This photo, showing a close view of Mercury, was taken by the space probe Mariner 10.

What is the surface of Mercury like?

Mercury is covered by dust. Craters scar its surface. Some of Mercury's craters are filled with lava. The lava may have come from volcanoes or from rocks that melted when they crashed to the planet's surface.

Because it has hardly any atmosphere, Mercury gets very hot—and very cold. In the daytime, Mercury's temperature can reach 800 degrees Fahrenheit! This is seven times hotter than the hottest desert on Earth. At night, the temperature drops to 300 degrees below zero Fahrenheit.

Mercury goes around the Sun about four times in every Earth year. A person 10 Earth-years old would have gone around the Sun more than 40 times if he or she lived on Mercury!

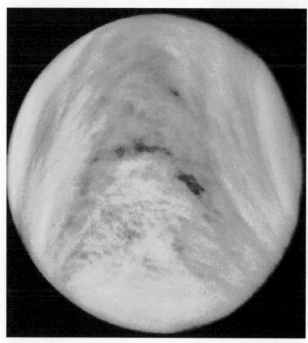

The surface of Venus is a scorching 900 degrees!

Which planet is closest to the Earth?

Venus is the planet closest to the Earth. It is also the second planet from the Sun. It takes 225 days to orbit the Sun. Venus is about the same size as Earth, but the atmosphere on Venus is much heavier than our own. On the surface of Venus, the pressure is 90 times that on Earth. That's equal to the pressure a diver would experience 264 feet under the ocean.

What is the surface of Venus like?

The surface of Venus cannot be seen because it is covered by pale yellow clouds. These clouds let in sunlight, but they do not let the heat out. Because the heat is trapped, Venus gets as hot as 900 degrees Fahrenheit.

One of the highest mountains in the solar system is on Venus. Called Maxwell Montes, it is more than a mile higher than Mount Everest!

MY FAVORITE COLOR IS RED!

Has anyone ever visited Venus?

Although people have not traveled to Venus, the United States and the Soviet Union have sent nearly two dozen spacecraft—called probes—to Venus. The first space probe to land on Venus in 1966 was quickly crushed by the planet's heavy atmosphere! Other space probes have sent back images of the dry, rocky planet. The first color television pictures were sent back in 1982. The pictures are sent by television because the probes themselves cannot return to Earth.

What is the "red planet"?

Mars has been called the red planet because it shines like a bright red star. It takes Mars 687 days to orbit the Sun. Scientists think that Mars is cold, dry, and lifeless. Temperatures on the planet range from 80 degrees Fahrenheit to 250 degrees below zero Fahrenheit.

41

Could humans breathe the air on Mars?

You could not breathe the air on Mars. There is no oxygen in it, and it is much thinner than the air on Earth. Since the air on Mars is so thin, it has very little pressure. On Mars, your blood would bubble the same way that a bottle of soda bubbles when the cap is opened.

MARS ROVER

Mars has the largest canyon in the solar system. It is many times longer than the Grand Canyon, and would stretch all the way across the United States!

What does the surface of Mars look like?

If you landed on Mars, you would see a rolling land covered by small rocks. Unmanned spacecraft have analyzed Martian soil— a rusty red dust. These spacecraft have also sent scientists photographs of volcanoes and riverlike canals, but there is no water in these canals.

What's the weather like on Mars?

Mars has four seasons— just as Earth does—but Martian seasons last twice as long because a year on Mars is twice as long as a year on Earth. No rain falls on Mars, but wild dust storms swirl across the planet each summer. White ice-caps spread over Mars's north and south poles in the winter. Photographs taken during that season show light patches of frost on one rocky plain.

JUPITER, SATURN, URANUS, NEPTUNE, AND PLUTO

What are the outer planets?

Jupiter, Saturn, Uranus, and Neptune are vast balls of gas circling in the solar system's outer reaches. These four planets are sometimes called the gas giants. They have small rocky centers surrounded by liquid and have thick clouds covering their surfaces. Beyond these four planets lies tiny, frozen Pluto.

Which is the largest planet?

Jupiter, the fifth planet from the Sun. All the other planets could easily fit inside it. Jupiter is larger than 1,300 Earths put together.

JUPITER'S RED SPOT

What is Jupiter's great red spot?

Scientists think this giant spot is a storm that moves on Jupiter's surface. The spot is 9,000 miles wide but in the past has been as large as 30,000 miles wide—much bigger than planet Earth. With a telescope, you can see the spot and follow it around Jupiter. People have been watching the great red spot for more than 300 years!

Jupiter's moon Io (EYE-oh) is the most explosive object in the solar system. Its volcanoes throw up enough material every 3,000 years to cover its own surface!

How long is a year on Jupiter?

One year on Jupiter is equal to almost 12 years on Earth. That's because Jupiter takes nearly 12 Earth years to orbit the Sun. Jupiter spins on its axis very quickly, however. It takes fewer than ten hours for this giant planet to make one turn!

SATURN'S RINGS

What is the second-largest planet in the solar system?

Saturn is the second-biggest planet. It takes almost 30 years to orbit the Sun. Saturn is known for the belt of colorful rings that move around its center.

What are Saturn's rings made of?

Saturn's rings, bands of small particles orbiting the planet, are made of countless pieces of ice, dust and ice-covered rock. These rings have a beautiful golden color when seen through a telescope.

The particles in Saturn's rings move at different speeds as they orbit the planet. The particles in the rings closer to Saturn move faster than the particles in the outer rings. The rings stretch over 40,000 miles, but they are only a few miles thick.

The planet Saturn is large but not very dense. If there were an enormous ocean in space, Saturn would float in it!

44

THE SEVENTH PLANET, MA'AM, IS DOC...NO, SNEEZY...NO, GRUMPY...NO...

What is the seventh planet from the Sun?

Uranus is the seventh planet from the Sun. It takes 84 years to orbit the Sun. Uranus is covered by methane gas, which gives it a bluish-green color. With temperatures probably reaching 300 degrees below zero Fahrenheit, Uranus is an icy world, far too cold for any living thing. Although it is the third-largest planet, Uranus appears very small, even in a telescope. It is more than 19 times farther from the Sun than the Earth is.

Uranus has a set of narrow rings made of boulder-sized chunks of the darkest material known in the solar system! These rings are so dark that scientists did not discover them until 1977!

Does Uranus have a twin?

Not really. When Neptune was discovered in 1846, scientists could tell that it was similar to Uranus. Both planets are very cold, both have rings, and both look green because of the methane gas in their atmospheres. The planets are similar in size, too. Each is about four times the size of Earth, but Uranus is a little bigger than Neptune. In spite of the similarities, however, the two planets are different enough so that scientists know they are not twins.

What is the weather like on Neptune?

Neptune is covered with layers of cold swirling clouds, so you would find lots of chilly windstorms on the planet. Scientists think these winds roar at speeds of 400 miles an hour! One big storm on the surface of the planet is about the size of Mars.

It takes Neptune, the eighth planet from the Sun, 164 Earth years to orbit the Sun.

The Voyager space probe sent back this picture of Neptune.

Which planet travels farthest from the Sun?

Pluto is the planet that travels farthest from the Sun. It is about 40 times farther from the Sun than the Earth is. It takes 248 Earth years for Pluto to complete one orbit around the Sun.

Pluto's path around the Sun is stretched out like an oval. Because of this odd orbit, Pluto is traveling closer to the Sun between 1979 and 1999 than it has traveled in other years. During that time, Neptune becomes the planet farthest from the Sun.

From Pluto, the Sun would look like a bright star among the other stars. Daylight on Pluto is like twilight here on Earth!

Which is the smallest planet?

Faraway Pluto is the smallest planet in our solar system. Scientists think it is only 930 miles wide—not even half the size of the Earth's Moon! Cold and dark, Pluto is often called a snowball in space!

ASTEROIDS, COMETS, AND METEORS

What are asteroids?

Asteroids are tiny planets in our solar system. There are thousands of them. Most of them have been discovered in the space between Mars and Jupiter. The largest asteroid is less than 500 miles wide. Most asteroids are chunks of rock that are less than one mile wide.

Through a telescope, asteroids look like stars. The word *asteroid* means "like a star."

The largest asteroid, named Ceres, is almost as big as the state of Texas!

Where did asteroids come from?

Scientists think that asteroids were formed the same time as the Earth and Sun. Asteroids are clumps of material that never grew big enough to become planets.

47

What is a comet?

A comet is a large ball of frozen gases, dust, and ice that glows brightly as it approaches the Sun. It travels in a long, cigar-shaped orbit around the Sun. Comets that can be seen without a telescope often have tails of glowing gases streaming out behind them. A comet's tail always points away from the Sun because the strong solar wind coming from the Sun blows the glowing gases backward off the comet.

A comet's tail can be more than a million miles long!

Why are some people afraid of comets?

Long ago, people were very frightened by comets. They believed that comets were signs of bad luck—sickness, war, floods, or even the end of the world. They were afraid that a comet would crash into the Earth and destroy it. Today, we accept comets as a part of our solar system. Comets are interesting to scientists because they are made of the same materials from which the planets were formed.

What is Halley's Comet?

Halley's Comet has appeared in our sky every 75 years since at least 240 B.C. In 1910, the Earth passed through the tail of Halley's Comet, but nothing bad happened because of it. In 1985 and 1986, Halley's Comet passed by the Earth again. Scientists from more than 50 countries used new instruments to collect new information. They learned that the nucleus, or head, of Halley's Comet is shaped like a peanut. It is about nine miles long and five miles wide.

What are meteors?

Meteors (MEE-tee-oars), often called shooting stars, are bright streaks of light speeding through the sky. A meteor appears when a bit of dust or rock that has been traveling through space vaporizes—heats up and turns to gas. The rock vaporizes because of the friction created as it speeds through the Earth's atmosphere. The glowing vapors are the streaks of light you see. A very brilliant meteor that leaves a shining trail as it streaks across the sky is called a fireball. Its trail lasts for as long as a minute or two.

What is a meteor shower?

A meteor shower happens when many meteors fall from the same place in the sky. A meteor shower can last for hours or even a few days. Scientists think the meteors of a meteor shower are millions of tiny pieces of a broken-up comet. These pieces fall into the Earth's air and burn up in it.

What is a meteorite?

A chunk of rock that does not completely burn up as it travels through the Earth's atmosphere is called a meteorite. It falls and lands on Earth.

Most meteorites have fallen in places where no one lives. In the past 100 years, only about 20 to 30 have fallen near people. There is no record that anyone has ever been seriously hurt by one.

A meteorite falling through Earth's atmosphere.

The world's largest meteorite landed in Namibia, Africa. It weighs about 60 tons— as much as nine elephants!

CHAPTER 6

Can stars make your wishes come true? Can you catch a falling star and put it in your pocket? From songs to stories to stargazing, the subject of stars has fascinated people since the beginning of time. What are stars really like? Well, let's go swing among them and we'll find out!

STAR-GAZING

STAR FACTS

What makes the stars shine?

Like our Sun, which is a star, stars shine with their own light because they are very hot. A lot of gases press down, causing great heat at the center of a star, and the star begins to shine.

The heart of a star reaches nearly 30 million degrees Fahrenheit. A grain of sand that hot would kill a person up to 100 miles away!

How big are the stars?

Stars are the biggest balls of gases scientists have found. They come in many sizes. Some stars, called dwarfs, are small—about the size of the Earth. Red dwarfs are small, cool, and faint. White dwarfs are very hot, but they appear faint in the sky because of their small size.

Our Sun is a middle-sized yellow star, more than a million times larger than the Earth. Many other stars are about the same size.

Some stars, called giants and supergiants, are much larger than our Sun. Orange giants and red supergiants are cool stars, but they are very bright, because of their huge size. Blue supergiants are the hottest, brightest stars of all.

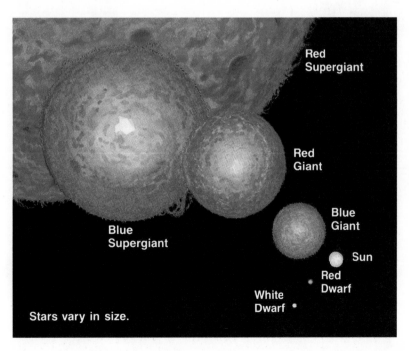

Stars vary in size.

The biggest supergiants known are 700 times larger than the Sun!

Why are stars different colors?

If you look at stars very carefully through a telescope, you will see that they have different colors. Their colors are caused by their temperature. Although all stars are very hot, some are hotter than others.

The hottest stars that you can see are blue-white. Yellow stars like the Sun are medium-hot. The coolest stars you can see are red.

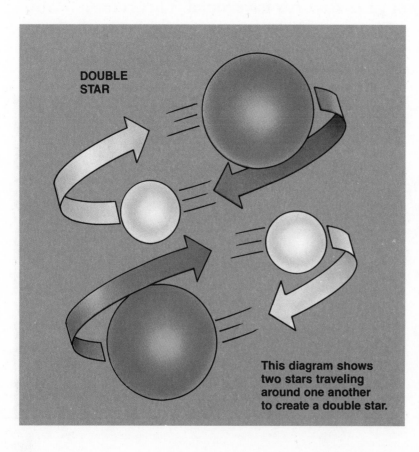

DOUBLE STAR

This diagram shows two stars traveling around one another to create a double star.

Is there such a thing as a double star?

Yes, there are thousands of them. A double star is made up of two neighboring stars that travel around each other. Most double stars look like single stars unless you look at them through a telescope.

One of the most mysterious double stars is called Epsilon Aurigae. These two stars revolve around each other every 27 years. Some scientists think that one star in this pair is the largest star ever known. If this star were placed in the middle of our solar system, its edge would reach as far as Uranus! Because it is so distant, this double star looks no brighter than other stars in the sky.

What is a star cluster?

A star cluster is made up of many stars that travel near each other. One popular star cluster, called Pleiades (PLEE-uh-deez), or the Seven Sisters, has about 400 stars in it. You can easily find this cluster in the night sky during the fall and winter without using a telescope. You will see five or six stars together in a clump. Through binoculars, you will see a dozen or more, and a telescope will show you hundreds!

Why do stars twinkle?

Stars don't really twinkle; they just seem to. There is a thick blanket of air around the Earth. The light coming from the stars must pass through this air. As the starlight passes through, it shifts, or moves about. This happens because of moisture in the air, changing air temperatures, and the constant movement of the air. When we see this shifting starlight, we think the stars are twinkling.

Where do the stars go in the daytime?

They don't go anywhere. They are always in the sky. But the Sun's bright light keeps you from seeing the stars during the day. In the evening, you can begin to see them again.

STARS FROM BEGINNING TO END

Where do stars come from?

Stars are born from huge clouds of gas and dust known as nebulas. If you traveled through the galaxy, you would sometimes see nebulas floating in the spaces between the stars. Stars begin to grow when a part of a nebula becomes very dense. This dense cloud contracts—gets smaller and hotter—until great heat is created at the center. Then the star begins to shine.

What happens when a star dies out?

During its lifetime, a star continues to contract. Eventually, a star burns up most of its material and begins to die. At first, the dying star begins to lose its gravity. This makes it swell up to an enormous size. Its surface starts to cool, and begins to glow red. At this stage, it is called a red giant.

Hundreds of millions of years may pass before the red giant collapses into a ball about the size of the Earth. This is called a white dwarf star. The white dwarf slowly gives off its last light and burns out. All that's left is a cold, black dwarf star.

Do all stars die out the same way?

Stars larger than our Sun may go through another stage before they die out. After they become red giants, their centers may explode. These great explosions are called supernovas. Supernovas send material flying through space.

What's left of the star becomes a small, dense object. Gravity squeezes the star down until it becomes a neutron star, a star having no electrical charge. It is only a few miles wide.

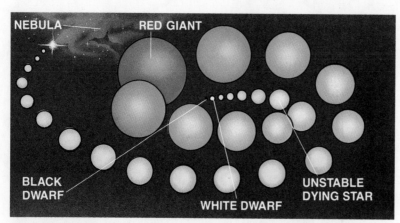

From its beginning as a huge cloud called a nebula to its end as a black dwarf star, a star goes through many phases. This process happens over billions of years.

What is a black hole?

Scientists believe that a black hole is formed when a dying star shrinks beyond the neutron star stage. While the star is burning, its heat and expanding gases help it keep its shape against the force of its own gravity, which is always pulling it inward. As the star cools, its gravity overpowers it, and the whole surface begins to get smaller and smaller.

Eventually, the star has no mass at all. Everything is pulled into its center and becomes invisible. Not even the tiny particles that make up light rays can escape the star's gravity. The star has become a black hole in space.

Will the same stars always be in the sky?

No. Old stars are always dying, and new stars are always being born. Some stars last a few million years. Others go on and on for hundreds of billions of years. But all stars someday either explode or get small and stop shining. At the same time, new stars keep forming from gas and dust in space.

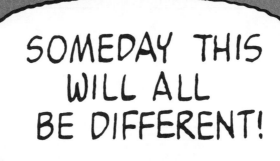

SOMEDAY THIS WILL ALL BE DIFFERENT!

Mapping Out the Stars

How many stars are there in the sky?

On a clear night, you can see about 2,000 stars just by looking up. You could see many thousands more with a small telescope. Giant telescopes allow you to see billions of stars.

As the Earth travels around the Sun, your view of the stars changes. If you stargaze monthly, you may see 6,000 different stars by the year's end.

Scientists keep building larger telescopes, enabling them to see farther into space. With each new telescope, scientists discover more stars. Some stars were too dim or too far away to show up in smaller telescopes. Since new stars are always being discovered, no one knows how many stars really exist.

LITTLE DIPPER

What is the Big Dipper?

The Big Dipper is a group of stars in the sky. If you could draw a line to connect them, you'd see that they look like the cup and handle of a water dipper.

Mizar (MY-zahr), the star at the bend of the Big Dipper's handle, is a double star. With a telescope, you can see its dim companion star.

The Big Dipper is one of many groups of stars that people have named for their shapes. We call these groups constellations (kon-stuh-LAY-shunz).

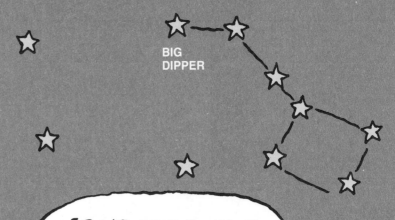

BIG DIPPER

IF WE COULD JUST FIND THE NORTH STAR, WE COULD FIND OUR WAY HOME.

What are the names of some other constellations?

You may have heard of the constellations Orion, the Hunter; Pegasus, the Winged Horse; or Ursa Major, the Great Bear.

LEO
THE LION

NORTH STAR

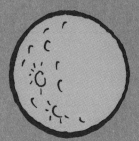

How can the stars help you if you are lost at night?

One very important star—the North Star—can help you, even though it's not the brightest star in the sky. You can find the North Star easily. The two stars in front of the Big Dipper point to it. If you face the North Star, you are facing north.

Some people learn the locations of other constellations to find the other directions. For example, in the winter, Orion, the Hunter, shows us the south. In the spring, Leo, the Lion, will be in the south, and this is where you find Scorpius in the summer. Stargazers can have fun finding the constellations and figuring out the directions.

IT MIGHT BE EASIER, IF THEY'D JUST USE MY MAP.

I'VE ALWAYS THOUGHT "SNOOPY" MEANT "GREAT DOG."

● After the Sun, the next-brightest star in our sky is Sirius, the Dog Star. It has that name because it is in the group of stars called Canis Major, which means Great Dog.

● Since 1974, a radio message beamed from the Arecibo radio telescope in Puerto Rico has been racing toward a cluster of stars called M13. Will there be creatures on M13 to receive and understand the message? Only time will tell, but if any creatures do receive our message and answer right away, the reply will come about 50,000 years from the time the message was sent. If anyone here is still listening!

● There is a kind of telescope, called a radio telescope, that can find stars even in the daytime! It picks up radio waves that come from outer space, the way your radio at home picks up radio waves from a station many miles away. All stars and some planets give off these waves. So do other faraway objects, such as galaxies and quasars. By listening to radio waves, scientists learn more about everything in outer space.

● Some scientists believe that the universe is expanding—getting bigger. They don't know how and why it's happening, but when they study the light from distant stars, they can see that other galaxies are racing away from ours.

Some scientists expect the universe to go on as it is for billions of years. After that, they think the last stars will shine and go out. The universe will become dark and cold.

Other scientists think that gravity will keep the galaxies from moving apart. They think the galaxies will fall together to form a glob of matter. This glob will explode in another big bang, and a new universe will begin!

● In 1963, radio waves were discovered coming from objects that look like bright stars but shine brighter than the brightest galaxies! What could they be? Scientists named these waves quasars. Quasars might be the earliest stages in the life of a galaxy. About 1,300 quasars have been discovered. They are the most distant objects that we can see. Some are 58,800,000 trillion miles away. That's 58,800,000,000,-000,000,000!

◆ IN THE ◆

NEXT VOLUME

Have you ever wondered what the first boats were like, or what a galleon is, or how an ice breaker works? You can find the answers to these questions and lots more in volume 10, *Boats and Things That Float—All Aboard!*